TAKING RESPONSIBILITY AND ACCOUNTABILITY

KEVIN EIKENBERRY

Participant Workbook

Pfeiffer
A Wiley Imprint
www.pfeiffer.com

Participant Workbook ISBN 978-0-470-50190-0
Facilitator's Guide Set ISBN 978-0-470-50557-1

Acquiring Editor: Holly J. Allen   Developmental Editor: Susan Rachmeler
Assistant Editor: Lindsay Morton   Production Editor: Michael Kay
Marketing Manager: Tolu Babalola   Manufacturing Supervisor: Becky Morgan
Director of Development: Kathleen Dolan Davies

Printed in the United States of America
Printing   10 9 8 7 6 5 4 3 2 1

Contents

THE COMPETENCIES OF REMARKABLE LEADERS

The Remarkable Leadership workshop series is based on the book *Remarkable Leadership: Unleashing Your Leadership Potential One Skill at a Time* and consists of twelve workshops, based on thirteen leadership competencies from the book. (There is no workshop for the first competency, learn continually, as that competency is embedded in all the workshops.) Although you may not be attending the full series of workshops, all thirteen competencies are listed next.

Remarkable Leaders . . .

1. Learn Continually

2. Champion Change

3. Communicate Powerfully

4. Build Relationships

5. Develop Others

6. Focus on Customers

7. Influence with Impact

8. Think and Act Innovatively

9. Value Collaboration and Teamwork

10. Solve Problems and Make Decisions

11. **Take Responsibility/Accountability**

12. Manage Projects and Processes Successfully

13. Set Goals and Support Goal Setting

WORKSHOP OBJECTIVES

After completing this workshop, you will

- Understand the importance of being personally accountable.

- Know what gets in the way of accountability.

- Recognize barriers to effective delegation.

- Know both the vicious and virtuous cycles of delegation.

- Know how to empower others.

OPENING QUESTIONS

Ponder, and then write your answers:

1. What do I hope to gain from this session?

2. What do I think of when I think of the word *accountable*?

SELF-ASSESSMENT

Here is a quick assessment to help you think about how accountable and responsible you are.

Use the following 1–7 scale on each question:

1 – Almost never	5 – Usually
2 – Rarely/Seldom	6 – Frequently
3 – Occasionally	7 – Almost always
4 – Sometimes	

I set an example of what I expect. ____

I follow through on promises and commitments. ____

I share work responsibilities with others. ____

I empower others. ____

I take personal responsibility. ____

Who are *they?*

Some things you can choose to be personally accountable for:

- Your beliefs and perspectives
- Your attitudes
- Your choices
- Your behaviors
- The commitments/promises you make
- The things for which you are responsible
- Your work—the tasks on your list

What is the difference between the first four and the last three?

■ Blame (also known as . . . commiserating, understanding, and explaining)

The Five Truths of Blame

- Blame is past focused, not solution focused.
- Blame doesn't allow for learning.
- Blame leads to passive inactivity.
- Blame is counterproductive.
- Blame is a waste of time.

■ Being a victim

SHARING RESPONSIBILITY— DELEGATING

Beliefs that can get in our way:

- "I don't have time to show someone else right now."

- "It's just faster to do it myself."

- "No one can live up to my quality standards." (Also expressed as "If you want something done right, do it yourself.")

- There is one best right way to do a task (and I know what that way is).

- The need to be indispensable.

- The need to be the hero.

- The desire to earn the mythical badge for being perpetually busy.

- The desire to look smart.

How people feel about delegation

THE VICIOUS CYCLE OF DELEGATION

1. I'm too busy to delegate, so I will try to get by.

2. I know I should delegate, but it is faster to do it myself.

3. I'm getting buried, so I better get Joe to do that.

4. I quickly hand off the task to Joe, not giving very clear directions or expectations because I don't have time, and he'll figure it out.

5. Joe realizes that he has been given work not because it will be challenging or will further his goals; in fact, it may be very clear to Joe that he has just been dumped on.

6. Joe's attitude about this task, given these observations, may not be the best. And while he'll get the job done, it might not be with the enthusiasm or final result that I hoped for. I may well get minimum performance levels.

7. This leads me to hesitate in delegating again.

How often do I get in this?

How can I get out?

THE VIRTUOUS CYCLE OF DELEGATION

1. I'm too busy to delegate, but I know that I have talented people who can do this task at least as well as I can.

2. I choose to invest the time to share this task—*and the responsibility for it*—with Joe.

3. It is going to take some time, but it will be time that reduces rework and helps Joe succeed, so I outline the goals, expectations, and boundaries with Joe and ask for his input and questions.

4. Joe takes the responsibility and integrates it into his work. He knows what success looks like and how this task fits into our overall goals.

5. Joe realizes that he has been given work that matters (even if the task is relatively small, he still sees how it fits into our overall success) and that it has been entrusted to him. While he might already be busy, he feels good about both the communication and the opportunity that has been presented to him.

6. Joe succeeds with the task—maybe the first time or maybe with some coaching—but he now owns the task and has built the skills necessary to do this task in the future, and the confidence to succeed with other new challenges as well.

7. And this overall success, even if I had to invest some more time upfront, leads me to want to share more responsibilities with Joe and others.

EMPOWERING OTHERS

What Is Empowerment?

Steps Toward Empowerment

1. You (again)
2. Boundaries
3. Resources
4. Latitude
5. The other person or group

What About the Rest of the Organization?

YOUR NOW STEPS

Being Personally Accountable

Here are some things you can do right now to strengthen your personal accountability. These are actions you can take at any time to instantly change your perspective and remind you that holding others accountable can only come with the foundation of personal accountability.

1. Think about the last person, group, or situation you blamed. Ask yourself what role you played in creating the situation.

2. Stop reading right now and say, out loud, "I am responsible!" five times. Then like the shampoo bottle says, "Rinse and repeat." Affirming your responsibility is one way to remind yourself and build your belief and resolve.

3. Decide to be accountable. There is likely one task or project on your plate now that has significant issues or challenges. Decide today to do what is in your power to make it work. Don't think about any of the obstacles other than to acknowledge and accept them. Don't give the obstacles power over you. Decide to make it happen.

Sharing Responsibility (Delegating)

These are actions you can take now or at any time to help you move into the virtuous cycle of responsibility sharing.

1. Devote some time to thinking about your beliefs and habits around delegating/sharing responsibility. Ask yourself what is your first (or maybe knee jerk) reaction to the idea of sharing responsibility?

2. Make a list of tasks or responsibilities that you could share for the benefit of yourself and others within your organization, those you will share those tasks with, and when that transfer can take place.

3. Pick one of those things and consciously start the virtuous cycle with someone or a team *today*. Recognize that if this is a very different approach than you have taken in the past, so you may want to explain your approach to those with whom you are sharing the responsibility. As you change habits, they will be changing their habits too.

Empowering Others

1. Look at the last situation where you feel you empowered others. Consider the factors outlined in this session (boundaries, resources, and latitude), and evaluate if and how well you provided these things. If you didn't do as well as you could have, schedule a time with those people to rectify those gaps.

2. Consider your own beliefs relating to empowerment. Be honest with yourself. If you truly want to empower others as we have discussed in this session and your beliefs are in alignment with that goal, spend some time thinking about your next steps. If you feel your beliefs are in alignment, use the steps in this section to match your actions to those beliefs.

3. Talk to those you have empowered (or will empower) about the concepts of personal responsibility. Share some of your reflections with them.

YOUR NEXT STEPS

1. Think back to your goals for being here (page 2). Reflect on what you have learned that you can apply to your situation.

2. Teach a colleague (or your team) this content as a way to solidify your own knowledge and understanding.

3. Be responsible for applying these concepts and ideas in your work and the rest of your life.

4. Ask yourself: "Which Now Steps will I apply *right now?*"

5. Take that action!

6. Commit to your daily application to lock in your learning and achieve greater results!

"We move toward our potential when we turn learning into action."

~Kevin Eikenberry

ADDITIONAL RESOURCES

More responsibility and accountability tips are available at www.RLBonus.com.

- To learn more about the five truths of blame, use the keyword "blame."

- To learn more about the victim-accountability choice, use the keywords "victim choice."

- For ten specific tips and techniques for increasing accountability in meetings, use the keywords "meeting accountability."